THEY CAME
FROM THE SKY

STEPHEN HARRIGAN

✠

THEY CAME FROM THE SKY

THE SPANISH ARRIVE IN TEXAS

A PREVIEW OF A FORTHCOMING
HISTORY OF TEXAS

UNIVERSITY OF TEXAS PRESS ⌄⌄ AUSTIN

Book designed by Derek George
Map designed by Molly O'Halloran

Requests for permission to reproduce material
from this work should be sent to:
Permissions
University of Texas Press
P.O. Box 7819
Austin, TX 78713-7819
http://utpress.utexas.edu/index.php/rp-form

∞ The paper used in this book meets the minimum requirements
of ANSI/NISO Z39.48-1992 (R1997) (Permanence of Paper).

LIBRARY OF CONGRESS
CATALOGING-IN-PUBLICATION DATA

Names: Harrigan, Stephen, 1948–, author.
Title: They came from the sky : the Spanish arrive
in Texas / Stephen Harrigan.
Description: First edition. | Austin : University of
Texas Press, 2017. | "A preview of a forthcoming history
of Texas." | Includes bibliographical references.
Identifiers: LCCN 2016043286
ISBN 978-1-4773-1294-0 (cloth : alk. paper)
ISBN 978-1-4773-1295-7 (library e-book)
ISBN 978-1-4773-1296-4 (nonlibrary e-book)
Subjects: LCSH: Texas—History. | Spaniards—Texas—
History. | Texas—Discovery and exploration.
Classification: LCC F386 .H27 2017 | DDC 976.4—dc23
LC record available at https://lccn.loc.gov/2016043286
doi:10.7560/312940

For my sons-in-law:

Rodney Randolph
Mike Guerrero
Zach Ernst

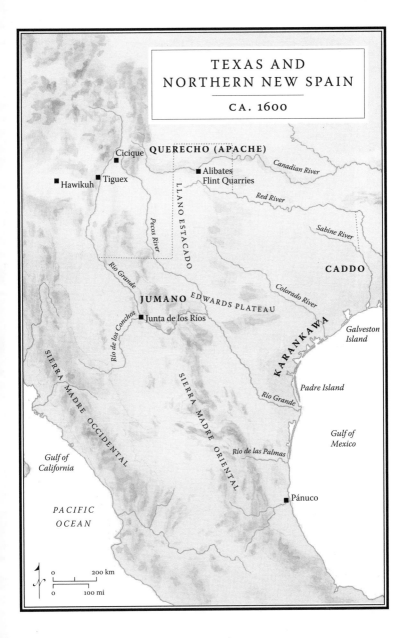

TEXAS AND NORTHERN NEW SPAIN

CA. 1600

Cicique

QUERECHO (APACHE)

Canadian River

■ Alibates
Flint Quarries

Red River

■ Hawikuh ■ Tiguex

LLANO ESTACADO

Pecos River

Sabine River

CADDO

Rio Grande

EDWARDS PLATEAU

Colorado River

JUMANO

Rio de los Conchos

■ Junta de los Ríos

SIERRA MADRE ORIENTAL

K A R A N K A W A

Galveston
Island

SIERRA MADRE OCCIDENTAL

Padre Island

Rio Grande

Gulf of
Mexico

Gulf of
California

Río de las Palmas

■ Pánuco

PACIFIC
OCEAN

0   200 km

0   100 mi

THE LANDSCAPE OF THE TEXAS Panhandle is called the High Plains for a reason. Even though the elevation in this part of Texas is less than four thousand feet, when you drive north from Amarillo on State Highway 136 the overwhelming flatness of the land creates a top-of-the-world sensation, a feeling that you are rising upon the surface of a brimming, borderless sea.

———

About twenty miles out of town, however, the land takes on texture. Shallow gullies and grassy declivities begin to appear, like ocean swells building under the stir of a gentle wind. Farther on, the change is dramatic. The flat land suddenly disappears entirely, replaced by a beautiful broken country where the Canadian River and its tributaries have sluiced deep below the limestone caprock into red Permian clay.

This is the site of the Alibates Flint Quarries. It's an important place, one of only two locations in Texas to be designated by the federal government as a national monument. But it's a safe guess that most of the people who find their way to the modest little visitor center at the bottom of a winding canyon road are drawn there less by the site's beckoning fame than by spur-of-the-moment curiosity. In truth, there isn't all that much to see, though what you do see you could spend a lifetime thinking about. Scattered over a series of windswept mesas above the Canadian River valley are more than a thousand pits that were dug into the rock by ancient toolmakers in search of high-quality flint for knives and spear and arrow points. The pits were only a few feet deep, and over the millennia most of them have filled up with soil and plant life, so that they register only as shallow depressions under a carpet of native prairie grasses and yellow broomweed flowers.

But pieces of the flint that was once quarried from these pits lie all around, flakes of agatized dolomite with intriguing striations and swirling colors, most characteristically a milky, muted shade of oxblood. There are natural outcroppings of this rock as well, big colorful boulders, but the paleo and archaic peoples who lived here appear to have mostly ignored the surface rock and dug with bone axes and hammerstones to get to the unweathered flint beneath the soil. They shaped it into what archaeologists call bifaces or trading blanks, hand-sized blocks of stone that they would carry back to their slab-housed villages or nomadic camps to be chipped and flaked into working implements. These unfinished pieces of flint were also currency in a trade network that flourished throughout North America for many thousands of years. In Texas, a state whose identity would become fused with the practice and ethos of business, with cotton, cattle, oil, real estate, shipping, aerospace, banking, and high tech, the production and distribution of flint was the first thriving enterprise.

Alibates flint went everywhere, carried along by ancient peddlers through draws and along riverbeds and game trails, traded as far away from the Southern High Plains as Minnesota and the Pacific coast. These quarries along the Canadian date back to the twilight of the last Ice Age. The people of that time and place shared the grasslands and forested savannas of early Texas with vanished megafauna like sloths and camels and saber-toothed cats and gigantic proto-armadillos. The earliest inhabitants shaped Alibates flint into the distinctively styled spear and projectile points that are classified today as Clovis, named for the town in New Mexico near which they were first discovered. Clovis points were long, often three

———

or four inches, and painstakingly flaked to create a groove on either side for fastening the point to a split shaft. Clovis-era hunters used these weapons to kill the great Columbian mammoths—less shaggy than their northern cousins but, at fourteen feet high, even taller—that flourished in the warming landscape below the retreating ice sheets.

The long-held archaeological conviction that Clovis artifacts represent the earliest inhabitants of North America—people who had threaded their way onto the continent when it was joined to Asia by an Ice Age landmass—has been challenged in recent years, the attacks originating from excavations at places like the Debra L. Friedkin Site forty miles north of Austin, in a rich transition zone between the rocky highlands of the Edwards Plateau and the deep black soil of the coastal prairie. Some of the tools found here—made out of local chert—lie deeper than the Clovis material. And they suggest an older technology that belonged to an earlier people, a people who had not yet developed Clovis innovations like fluted spear points, and who had taken up residence in the Americas several thousand years before archaeologists had thought humans first lived here.

Between this earliest estimate of human habitation in Texas to the first encounters with Europeans in the early sixteenth century lies an unimaginable stretch of deep time: fifteen thousand years, five hundred generations of people for whom we have no tangible history, not a single name of a person or even a tribe. We know them only by buried artifacts in the strata of flood deposits and trash pits, by mementoes or offerings left behind in their graves, by the puzzling imagery they carved or painted on rock walls, and by the traces of illness, old wounds, and lifelong wear visible in their bones and teeth.

Four hundred and fifty miles due south of the Alibates Flint Quarries, in the desert canyon lands where the Pecos River meets the Rio Grande, are hundreds of rock shelters carved out of the limestone by Pleistocene rivers. The shelters are sweeping and commodious, natural gathering places for people seeking refuge from harsh weather or perhaps in search of panoramic vistas from which to contemplate their place in creation. Excavations in the soil of the shelter floors have revealed a great deal of information about how these early inhabitants lived. There are sandals and bedding woven from lechuguilla fibers, weapons and implements demonstrating the advances of Stone Age technology, the remains of earth ovens where the fibrous bulbs of sotol plants were baked for days to make them edible. But when you look up at the painted rock art on the ceilings and walls of the shelters all you see is what might never truly be known, the consciousness and cosmology of a people who long ago moved on from these painted canyons.

The pictographs feature strange provocative forms: elongated, vaguely human shapes with antlers or rabbit ears sprouting from their featureless heads, sometimes rising with outstretched arms in a posture that suggests flight or resurrection from some dark underworld. There are bat-like creatures and headless entities in the shapes of rectangles or gourds, and scattered renderings of dead animals impaled by arrows or atlatl darts. There are waving serpentine lines and insect shapes and spiky paramecium blobs that some scholars believe represent the peyote buttons that might have been the means of accessing an archaic spiritual realm. These tableaux have been degraded in modern times by vandalism and pollution and by the humidity created by the construction of the nearby Amistad Reservoir, but their hallucinogenic power is still very much alive. They were painted around the same time the Egyptian pharaohs were building their tombs in the Valley of the Kings, and they hint at a similarly complex belief system, one of soul-journeying and form-shifting and travels to and from mysterious otherworlds.

The canyons of the Lower Pecos appear not to have been continuously inhabited. Rock shelters were abandoned when the population moved on, perhaps in response to climate changes and the rise of better hunting and gathering opportunities elsewhere. After long stretches of time, other sorts of people would move in, people with different tools and aesthetics, who painted the rock in accordance with a different understanding of humanity's origins and the soul's destination. The already ancient designs left behind by the previous occupants might have been as inscrutable to them as the Sphinx was to Alexander the Great.

All over the region that would become Texas, throughout the unchronicled centuries, populations shifted as resources surged or dwindled, or as one tribe or band violently displaced another. (At the Harrell site in North Central Texas, there are mass graves containing human bones with embedded arrow points, and skulls whose missing mandibles were probably carried away as war trophies.) The nomadic people of the plains followed the mammoth migrations, and when the mammoths were gone—casualties of climate change, human predation, or both—they hunted an ancestral species of big-boned, big-horned ruminant that dominated the grasslands and eventually evolved into the modern-day bison. The expressions of human culture evolved as well, from simple thrusting spears to atlatls to bows and arrows, from designs scratched onto pebbles to intricate ornamental pottery. In the forests and deep-soiled prairies to the east, far from the deserts and drought-prone plains that lie above the massive rampart of uplifted limestone known as the Balcones Escarpment, a settled farming and village life began to take hold. This part of Texas lay at the western edge of the Mississippian culture that arose in the southeastern woodlands of the continent in the centuries before the arrival of Europeans. The best-known people here were the Caddos of the Hasinai Confederacy, known to the Spanish as the Tejas. They built great ceremonial centers whose elaborate earthen temples and burial mounds can still be traced in the hummocky contours of the East Texas landscape.

By the beginning of the sixteenth century, Texas was well-populated with indigenous peoples living in nomadic family groups or in settled villages that, according to one early Spanish estimate, contained "tens of thousands." They spoke a bewildering spectrum of languages and were splintered into so many tribes and bands that Juan Mendoza, exploring Texas in 1784, counted up sixty-four "nations" in attendance at some sort of rendezvous or trading fair on the Colorado River near present-day Ballinger.

ON THE GULF OF MEXICO LIVED A people that came to be known as the Karankawas. They were divided into five bands spread out along the margins of the Texas coast. Karankawas moved with the seasons. They spent the summers hunting and harvesting on the mainland prairies, and in the fall and winter they set up camp along the bay shores or paddled their dugout canoes across the lagoons to the string of low-lying barrier islands that protected the inland waters from the open gulf. They moved seaward to take advantage of the spawning seasons of drum and redfish and speckled trout, catching the fish in weirs and nets or through deadly accurate use of their distinctively long bows. Karankawas were famously tall; everyone who encountered them remarked on it. They were tattooed and mostly naked, their lower lips sometimes pierced with short lengths of cane, their skin glistening with the alligator grease they employed to ward off mosquitoes. They made pottery and painted designs on it with black beach tar. They lived in willow-framed huts that could be gathered up and moved quickly as they followed the food sources season to season.

On a freezing November day in 1528, on some narrow windswept stretch of—or near—Galveston Island, a hunting party of three Karankawa men encountered a shocking apparition. It was a man, or at least something like a man, carrying a pot he had stolen from their village while all the people were away. He had taken some fish as well, and was either carrying or being followed by one of the village dogs. The stranger was starving and haggard. His skin was oddly pale, his hair and beard matted.

———

His emaciated body shivered beneath the few loose rags that covered it. He looked back at the Karankawas, but ignored their attempts to communicate with him and kept walking toward the desolate ocean beach. When he reached it, the Karankawas held back a little, staring in amazement. There were forty other men there, sprawled in the sand around a driftwood fire. Near them, half-buried in the sand where it had been violently driven in by the waves, was some sort of crude vessel, a thirty-foot-long raft of lashed pine logs, with a rough-hewn mast and spars and a disintegrating sail made out of sewn-together shirts.

Within a half hour, another hundred or so Karankawa warriors had arrived to gawk at the castaways. They did not seem to be a threat, since they had no weapons and most of them were too weak to stand. Finally two of the men rose from the sand and staggered over to the Indians. The one who seemed to be the leader did his best to communicate by signs that they meant no harm, and he presented them with trading goods, some beads and bells that had somehow survived as cargo during whatever disastrous voyage had just taken place.

The Karankawas made signs that they intended to return the next morning with food. They made good on their promise, bringing fish and cattail roots, and kept coming back to feed the men for several days. One evening they returned to find the strange visitors in even more desperate shape. During the day they had tried to resume their ocean journey, digging their raft out of the sand, stowing their clothes on board, and paddling out toward the open gulf. Not far from shore, they had been hit by a wave, and the raft had capsized and been pounded apart against the sandbars that run parallel to the Texas shoreline. Three men had drowned, and the survivors were all now naked and so close to death from exposure that the Karankawas broke out into loud ritualistic lamentations. Then, realizing that the men would not survive the night, they got to work, some of them running off to build a series of bonfires to warm the castaways en route to their villages, others bodily picking up the starving, freezing men and carrying them to shelter.

T HE KARANKAWAS WERE NOT A MARI-time people. They probed the bays and lagoons and paddled back and forth from the mainland to the barrier islands, but the open Gulf of Mexico remained a mysterious immensity beyond the reach of their dugout canoes. And far to the east, beyond the straits of Florida, there was a much greater sea of whose existence they might only have heard through unreliable stories passed along by other tribes. It was from the far side of this unknown ocean that the ghostlike men trying to revive themselves around the fires in the natives' willow-framed lodges had come. They were adventurers from Spain, part of an epochal wave of expansion and exploration generated by the completion of a struggle that had lasted seven centuries, the Christian reconquest of the Muslim-dominated Iberian Peninsula. By 1492, King Ferdinand and Queen Isabella, whose marriage had allied the Catholic kingdoms of Aragon and Castile, had conquered Granada, the last stronghold of Al-Andalus, the name by which Muslim Spain had long been known. That same year, they financed Columbus's first voyage of discovery, and his landfall in the West Indies gave Spain a new horizon toward which to direct its surging national confidence, and a new world to exploit.

The men who had washed up naked on this forsaken beach were, in all likelihood, the first Europeans ever to set foot in Texas. (A Spanish expedition led by Alonso Álvarez de Pineda had sailed along this coast in 1519 and had drawn a map of it, but there is no record of them going ashore.) They came thirty-six years after Columbus, when the Spanish colonization and conquest of the Caribbean Basin and of Mexico was well under way, and when the invasion of the Inca empire in Peru was about to begin. The doorway to two continents had been breached, and it was crowded with men of rampant ambition trying to beat each other through it. Some of these men were *adelantados*, licensed by the Crown to risk their own fortunes in order to find and subjugate new lands. If successful, if their ships didn't go down in a hurricane or run aground against uncharted shoals, if they didn't starve or die of disease or get killed by the native inhabitants they had come to conquer, they would be granted titles and far-reaching administrative powers and inexhaustible wealth.

Others, like Hernán Cortés, made up in bravado what they lacked in official sanction. In 1518, Cortés was commissioned by Diego Velázquez, the governor of Cuba, to explore the newly discovered coast of Yucatán, from which two previous expeditions had returned with reports of sophisticated cities with towering stone temples and a casual abundance of gold. But Velázquez had never really trusted Cortés, and as he began to suspect his commander of being a competitor and not a subordinate partner, he withdrew the commission and even ordered his arrest. But Cortés was too fast and too crafty and the order came too late. By February of 1519 his fleet of eleven ships had already sailed, heading westward across the Yucatán channel toward the Mexican Gulf Coast. There Cortés and his men encountered the unimaginable and proceeded to accomplish the unthinkable. Tenochtitlán, the capital of the Aztec empire, was as proud and populous as any city in Europe. To the Spaniards who beheld it after fighting their way inland from the coast, it was a sprawling, glittering, dreamlike metropolis, a place whose temple pyramids and strange sculptures and frescoes were startling in their alien beauty, and whose culture of human sacrifice—of ripped-out hearts and priests with blood-caked hair—struck their fervently Catholic minds as a devil's pageant of horror. In only a little over two years, with a fighting force that began with fewer than six hundred men and sixteen horses but that was exponentially increased by Cortés's dynamic diplomacy among subjugated tribes primed to rebel against Aztec domination, the Spaniards had conquered Tenochtitlán and begun the work of tearing down its temples, determined to erase this wondrous abomination of a city from human memory.

There was no Aztec grandeur on the Texas coast, a thousand miles north of Tenochtitlán, where the Karankawa bands pieced together a subsistence existence following the cycles of spawning fish and ripening fruits and nuts. And they could hardly have considered the desperate wraiths they had taken into their village as conquerors. Unlike Cortés, these Spaniards had no ships, no armor, no weapons, no intimidating beasts like the never-before-seen horses. But a year and a half earlier, these men had sailed pridefully out of the harbor in Seville and down the Guadalquivir River into the open Atlantic, part of an expedition made up of five ships and six hundred people. The expedition had a grant from King Ferdinand's grandson Charles, now King of Spain and Holy Roman Emperor, to conquer and populate all the land from the northern border of Cortés's Mexican possessions to the Florida peninsula.

———

The voyage was led by a ruthless soldier and tireless schemer named Pánfilo de Narváez. Narváez had been Diego Velázquez's sword arm in the conquest of Cuba, where he watched impassively from horseback as his men butchered the inhabitants of a village on the Caonao River. In 1520, Velázquez, still fuming over Cortés's usurpation of his Yucatán mission, put together a powerful fleet of eighteen ships to intercept Cortés, throw him in irons, and neutralize any claim he tried to make for the plundered wealth of Mexico. Narváez, who had served Velázquez so cruelly well in Cuba, commanded the expedition. When Narváez's armada landed, Cortés had already entered Tenochtitlán, where in an unnervingly brazen stroke he had taken the Aztec leader Moctezuma hostage in his own palace. Even though his position was exquisitely vulnerable, he left several hundred men behind in the city and marched the rest of his army to the coast. Cortés swiftly outwitted and outfought Narváez, peeling away some of his officers with bribes and overpowering his force in a surprise nighttime attack.

Narváez lost an eye in the fight and spent two and a half years in a fetid dungeon while Cortés finished conquering Mexico with the help of the soldiers Narváez had brought to arrest him.

But his career still held an even more disastrous third act. Once he was released from prison, Narváez sailed to Spain, where he spent five years lobbying Charles V and the Council of the Indies for permission to "explore, conquer, populate and discover all there is to be found of Florida." The name Florida at that time meant the entire sweeping coastline of the Gulf of Mexico from Mexico's Río de las Palmas to the Florida Keys. In 1527, Narváez's petition to become an *adelantado* was finally granted, and he set out across the Atlantic with five ships bearing six hundred men and women—soldiers, colonists, slaves, and priests—to claim and somehow try to possess an unknown part of the world that was four times larger than Spain itself.

The fleet stopped in Cuba, where a hurricane destroyed one of Narváez's ships and drowned sixty men, and where the surviving vessels ran aground

—

onto shoals and encountered more storms once they were under sail again. But the hard luck had barely started. From Havana, Narváez sailed due westward for the Río de las Palmas, on the central coast of Mexico, which was the western boundary of his vast territorial claim. He never reached it. After a month at sea, caught up in the fast-moving swirl of the Gulf Stream which turned out to be bearing the ships in the opposite direction, and with food running low and horses dying in the holds, the fleet made landfall on the western coast of Florida, all the way across the Gulf of Mexico from its planned landing site.

Even though they were fifteen hundred miles away from the Río de las Palmas, the thoroughly disoriented Spaniards still thought they had nearly reached their destination. They encountered Indians who encouraged them to believe that there was a great kingdom, full of gold, not far to the west. Narváez decided to reconnoiter on land, taking three hundred men and sending the rest of the expedition ahead on the ships to wait for them further up the coast. The two parts of the divided expedition never saw each other again. Narváez and his land party spent four months wandering lost and starving through nearly impassable swamps and forests, blundering into sieges and skirmishes with the native inhabitants. Desperate and unable to find the ships with which they were supposed to rendezvous, they killed and ate their horses, and set about the almost impossible task of building five seaworthy vessels that would allow them to set sail again for the Río de las Palmas. They still believed the river lay somewhere just along the coast, and once they found it they could make their way to Pánuco, Mexico's northernmost Spanish settlement. The two hundred and fifty men who were left—fifty had died of disease or drowning or starvation—constructed a crude forge and melted down their crossbows and stirrups in order to make axes to chop down trees and nails to hold their wooden rafts together.

The men were at sea on their rafts for a month and a half. They sailed westward along the Florida

Panhandle, then across the mouth of the Mississippi. They were nearly dead from dehydration when the rafts finally drifted apart, strung out along the length of the Texas coast. Most of the men made it to shore somewhere. But Pánfilo de Narváez, the *adelantado* whose claim to all the lands of Florida was now a pathetic presumption, was last seen drifting out into the gulf on his raft.

✝

A S THE MEN WHO HAD BEEN TAKEN into the Karankawa village on Galveston Island began to revive somewhat around the fire pits, watching the Karankawas dance all night in a frighteningly ambiguous celebration, they grew alarmed. In the months since leaving Cuba, they had encountered numerous native peoples whose reaction to their presence had been mercurial, unreadable, and often violent. And they had heard the stories of what had befallen other Spaniards in Mexico, men who had been captured and sacrificed to alien gods, then flayed so thoroughly and expertly that their comrades, finding their skins strung up on temple walls, were still able to recognize their boneless, bearded faces. They were convinced that something similar was in store for them. But as the days passed the Karankawas continued to treat them as unfortunate refugees and not as captives to be sacrificed.

The leader of the Spaniards, the man who had approached the Karankawas on the beach, asking for help and offering trade goods, was Álvar Núñez Cabeza de Vaca. He was probably in his mid-thirties, from a distinguished family with ties to the royal court. He had been a functionary in the houses of Andalusian dukes when he was younger but had spent most of his career as a soldier, fighting the French at the Battle of Ravenna and insurrectionists in Castile. On Narváez's expedition, he was the royal treasurer, whose mission was to ensure that the Crown received its share of any New World wealth.

―――

But there was no longer any need for wealth to be accounted for, and only a very slim possibility of surviving. Two of the five rafts had drifted well south of the island that Cabeza de Vaca and his companions came to call Malhado—"ill fortune"—and the men on those rafts were either killed outright by Indians or died of starvation and exposure. Two other rafts had landed east of Cabeza de Vaca on Malhado, bringing the total number of survivors on the island to eighty or so. But most of the men were too sick or malnourished to survive, and within weeks only sixteen were left. Five of the Spaniards from Cabeza de Vaca's raft had stayed behind on the beach rather than face the horrors they imagined waiting for them in the village. Starving there, they quickly turned to cannibalism. When the Indians discovered this, the relationship between the castaways and their hosts quickly began to deteriorate. The Karankawas appear to have practiced ritualistic cannibalism against their enemies, but they could not abide the idea of human beings actually eating each other

———

for food. This is a resonant historical irony, given that they have long been saddled with the reputation of being rapacious man-eaters themselves. ("Cannibal Indians," intones the narrator of a 1960 Texas Department of Public Safety travelogue, "used to waylay shipwrecked sailors and then chase them up and down the island one at a time as the menu indicated.")

The Karankawas watched the Spaniards die, and then they began to die themselves. During the course of that terrible winter, over half the Indians on the island perished. So many died so suddenly that the Indians' mourning customs—elaborate burials and cremations, the drinking of water mixed with the pulverized bones of the deceased, a year of ritual weeping at every sunrise—become impossible to carry out. Undone with grief and bewilderment, they assumed the Spaniards were murdering them through some sort of dark magic. And there was indeed an invisible lethal force at work, one that had already ravaged the indigenous people of the Indies and in years to come

———

would bring unimaginable catastrophe to native populations throughout the Americas: Old World pathogens like smallpox and measles, for which the Karankawas had no immunity.

The traumatized Indians who survived this initial epidemic spared the Spaniards' lives, but grudgingly. Having first taken their visitors in out of charity, they now made them slaves. Cabeza de Vaca and the others were continually beaten and threatened, and forced to dig up roots from the freezing saltwater marshes with their bleeding fingers. In the spring of 1529, thirteen of the Spaniards managed to escape from Malhado and make their way south along the coast, determined to somehow still reach the Spanish settlement at Pánuco. Cabeza de Vaca was too ill to join the trek, but when he recovered he too fled the island for the mainland, where he fell in with a tribe called the Charrucos, who treated him better and put him to work as a long-distance peddler. They sent him off on long solitary trading missions deep into the heart of the country, where he bartered for hides and flint, offering sea shells and pearls from the coast in exchange. Traveling alone in an alien land, in constant peril from hunger and thirst and hostile weather, he was nevertheless exhilarated by his liberation from his enslavement on Malhado, and by a newfound sense of purpose and confidence.

This occupation served me very well, because practicing it, I had the freedom to go where I wanted, and I was not constrained in any way nor enslaved.

The words are from a book Cabeza de Vaca wrote that has come to be known as *La relación* (The account). Acknowledging in a preface that its contents would be "very difficult for some to believe," he published the book in Spain in 1542, with a second edition thirteen years later. It's one of the world's rare books, but there are places, like the Wittliff Collections at Texas State University in San Marcos, where you can ask for it and hold it in your own hands. The double-headed eagle of

———

Charles V is on the frontispiece, the ancient rag paper is pleasingly supple and tactile, the pages so dense with sixteenth-century typography there are hardly any margins. *La relación* is the first book ever written about Texas. It's a work of survival literature, of natural history, of anthropology, of what must have seemed to readers of the time as extraterrestrial travel.

The book recounts the doomed voyage from Cuba to Florida and the desperate attempt to sail on to the Río de las Palmas on rafts, as well as the almost six years Cabeza de Vaca spent wandering with his trade goods through the interior of Texas and up and down its desolate coast. He wrote about the strange and frightening customs he witnessed among the people he encountered—their theatrical weeping and fluid gender roles, the way that unwanted female babies were sometimes buried alive or fed to dogs, the contrasting tenderness toward children and unstoppable grief when they died. He wrote about "vipers that kill men when they strike" and about great herds of "cows" that ranged down from the north, creatures with long fur and curved horns like Moorish cattle—the first-ever written reference to bison.

For most of those years he was separated from his fellow Spaniards. But in 1533, in the pecan forests near the mouth of San Antonio Bay where all the bands of the region migrated in the spring to gather nuts, Cabeza de Vaca encountered what was left of the group that had set out years earlier for Pánuco when he was too sick to join them. Of those thirteen men, only three were still alive, and their long odyssey to the Spanish settlement had been interrupted by years of captivity and servitude among the various tribes that inhabited the coastal prairies of South Texas. Two of the men, Andrés Dorantes and Alonso del Castillo, were, like Cabeza de Vaca, soldiers of noble rank. The third is referred to in *La relación* by the diminutive version of the Christian name—Esteban—that had been assigned to him after he was captured by slavers, probably somewhere in sub-Saharan Africa, and sold in the markets of Morocco or Spain.

—

He had come to the New World as the property of Dorantes. Now, along with his master, Estebanico was a new sort of slave, in bondage not just to the inscrutable mores of the alien peoples he had encountered but to the imprisoning wilderness all around him.

It had been six years since their rafts came ashore on Malhado, but the four men still dreamed of reaching the Spanish settlement at Pánuco. It would be two more frustrating years before they could coordinate their escape. They finally slipped away in the spring of 1535, during the time of year when the native groups scattered throughout the region moved south toward the Nueces River for the annual harvest of the prickly pear fruits that grew there in staggering abundance.

The four escapees trekked through an inhospitable landscape of cactus, thorny brush, and shadeless, spindly trees. Though the Spanish outpost of Pánuco lay on the coast three hundred miles south, they kept well inland, where they had learned from experience the people tended to be more welcoming to strangers. They came to the Rio Grande, shallow enough to wade across but, as Cabeza de Vaca wrote, wider than the Guadalquivir down which Narváez's impressive fleet had first sailed.

The country was harsh but the four castaways were no longer wretched. They had learned the languages and the customs of the people among whom they had passed, and they were conditioned to hardship and unsurprised by it. Also, they were beginning to emerge from servitude into celebrity.

Back on Malhado, the castaways had been pressed into service as healers. Cabeza de Vaca and the others were nervous practicing an art about which they knew nothing, whose stakes were high and whose results they could not control. But the Karankawas threatened to let them starve if they didn't comply. So the Spaniards cautiously began, adding their own Christian flourishes—the sign of the cross, the Lord's Prayer—to the native repertoire of ritual healing. The two forms of magic turned out to be compatible enough for at least some healing to take place, and the castaways, even

———

though they were still slaves, began to take on the power of shamans.

By the time they crossed the Rio Grande they had developed a surging reputation. Each tribe they encountered had heard of their cures, and as they ventured deeper into Mexico they accumulated a constant following of people eager to see the foreigners and witness their miracles. Often Estebanico went ahead as a kind of mysterious herald, the inhabitants startled and mesmerized by his black skin.

They were only about two hundred miles from Pánuco, the Spanish province that had been the focus of all their dreams of salvation, when they turned west, moving far away from the coast and toward the peaks of the Sierra Madre. No longer starving, no longer enslaved, they now enjoyed a superhuman status among the people they met, who followed them from one village to the next in processions that grew to number in the thousands. If in the previous years they had felt forsaken by God, perhaps now they sensed his guiding hand as they blew their healing breath over the bodies of the afflicted or even performed surgery on them with flint knives and sutured the incisions with deer-bone needles. It seems plausible that they turned away from the coast and moved deeper into the interior out of a reawakened sense of discovery. Along the way they encountered things that encouraged them: an intricately worked copper bell with a human face, cotton blankets, baskets of maize. All of this indicated that, if they kept going, they might still fulfill one of the original purposes of the Narváez expedition—to discover cities of vast wealth like the one Cortés had found in the Valley of Mexico.

They found further hints of what might lie ahead when they turned north again and recrossed the Rio Grande back into what is now Texas, many miles upstream from where they had first crossed it. Beyond, where the Rio Grande met the Conchos in the Junta de los Ríos, near where the town of Presidio is today, they entered the fertile country of the Jumanos, an agricultural people

———

who lived in flat-roofed stone apartments—"the first dwellings we saw that had the semblance and appearance of houses."

They lingered with the Jumanos and then kept on, believing that "going the route of the setting sun we would find what we desired." They were constantly followed by a huge crowd of native disciples. "They always accompanied us," Cabeza de Vaca wrote, "until they left us handed over to others. And among all these peoples, it was taken for certain that we came from the sky." And it was in the sky, the Spaniards preached to the Indians, that their God lived. If they believed in him too, if they obeyed his teachings, things "would go very well for them."

But things did not go well for the people who accompanied Cabeza de Vaca. After following the Rio Grande north for several weeks, the party turned southwest, still moving in the direction of the setting sun, searching for the cities of great wealth and sophistication they had come to believe lay beyond the horizon. They made their way through the Chihuahuan Desert, through the mountain passes of the western Sierra Madre, down to the coastal plateaus of the Gulf of California. In a little more than six months, they had walked across the continent of North America. And now they were among people who were not naked hunter-gatherers, but who lived in stable houses and grew crops and wore shirts and robes of finely woven cotton. By this time, the desperate men from Malhado had reached their highest level of spiritual influence. In one village, they were given a gift of six hundred deer hearts. Mothers who had just given birth presented their infants to the healers so that they could be blessed with the sign of the cross.

They met an Indian wearing a necklace fashioned from the buckle of a Spanish sword belt. This could only mean that the countrymen they had been seeking in the wilderness for eight years were at last somewhere nearby. Cabeza de Vaca and the others pressed anxiously on, reassuring their Indian followers, telling them they would intercede with any Christians so that "they should not kill them or take them as slaves."

But they moved through a country now that had been devastated—villages burned and almost deserted, the few remaining people sick and starving, the rest fled to the mountains or taken captive. Finally, at the end of Cabeza de Vaca's unimaginably long road, he encountered the cause of this havoc. One day he found himself staring up at four Spaniards mounted on horseback, "who experienced great shock upon seeing me so strangely dressed and in the company of Indians. They remained looking at me a long time, so astonished that they neither spoke nor managed to ask me anything." The bearded, helmeted men looking down in stupefaction from their horses were part of a slave-hunting expedition in the service of Nuño de Guzmán, the rapacious governor of the Mexican province of Nueva Galicia.

It was 1536, a time when a fervent argument was raging over the "capacity" of the people the Spanish had discovered inhabiting the new world. Were they some low, half-bestial variant of humanity, or had God given them souls that might be brought to salvation, and slumbering intellects that could be awakened and made to understand the gospels and the mysteries of faith? Passionate, conscience-torn priests like Antonio de Montesinos, who in 1511 shocked the conquistadors of Hispaniola by asking, "Are these Indians not men? Do they not have rational souls?," and Bartolomé de las Casas, who as a young man had witnessed Narváez's rampages in Cuba, had begun to win the argument, at least in the courts of philosophy. And a year later, in 1537, Pope Paul III would issue the bull Sublimis Deus, which decreed that "Indians and all other people who may later be discovered by Christians, are by no means to be deprived of their liberty or the possession of their property . . . nor should they be in any way enslaved." But such distant moral declarations were only limp pieties on the ground in New Spain, where men like Guzmán needed slaves to work their extensive lands and their silver and gold mines, and to export to the Antilles in exchange for livestock and other commodities.

Cabeza de Vaca pleaded for the freedom of the Indians who were traveling with his party, but the Spanish captain, interested only in enslaving them, sent the castaways off under armed guard to the town of Culiacán, where they could not interfere. A few months later they arrived in Mexico City, where they astonished Viceroy don Antonio de Mendoza and Hernán Cortés himself with their story of having survived the doomed Narváez expedition and managing to stay alive for eight long years in a vast wilderness realm no other European had ever seen. The wanderers had trouble readjusting to Spanish life, feeling weighed down by their borrowed clothes and unable to sleep comfortably anywhere except on the ground. And Cabeza de Vaca's conscience—expanded by the experience of being saved, enslaved, and finally venerated by an ever-changing cast of native peoples—was no longer a natural fit with the hubristic spirit of conquest.

✝

THE GHOSTLY REAPPEARANCE OF Cabeza de Vaca and his companions startled the inhabitants of New Spain and set in motion a new wave of exploration. If there were civilizations far to the north capable of fabricating copper bells and weaving fine cotton, wasn't it logical to assume that somewhere in this "Tierra Nueva" there might be another golden city like Tenochtitlán? In fact, there might be seven such cities, a legend that had taken root in the Iberian imagination as far back as the 700s, when it was believed that seven bishops had sailed away from the Moorish conquest of Spain and founded Christian cities far from Europe in some unknown land beyond the Ocean Sea.

Viceroy Mendoza tried to recruit the three white survivors of the Narváez expedition to retrace their steps northward in search of the seven cities, but for various reasons all of them turned him down.

In the end there was only one man available who knew anything about the country and the people who lived north of Nueva Galicia. Though in the wilderness he had been effectively emancipated by the leveling hardships he had shared with his fellow castaways, Estebanico was now a slave again, and he was ordered into service as the guide for a new *entrada*. He may very well have welcomed the mission, given the swagger he showed on the expedition, which was led by a Franciscan cleric named Fray Marcos de Niza.

Accompanied by two Castilian greyhounds and bearing a talismanic gourd decorated with feathers and rattlesnake rattles to present to the chieftains he met, Estebanico scouted far in advance of Fray Marcos's main party, following rumors that "the greatest thing in the world" lay ahead. Both Estebancio and Marcos became increasingly confident that they were soon to encounter a land called Cíbola where there were indeed seven cities, splendid cities where the people lived in towering houses made of stone and inlaid turquoise and slept on canopied beds.

When he arrived at Hawikuh, the first of these cities, Estebancio made a fatal miscalculation. The presentation of his ceremonial gourd was refused and the inhabitants—probably alerted by stories of Spanish atrocities in Nueva Galicia—warned him and his large Indian entourage not to approach the city. But Estebanico had spent so many years as a celebrated guest among multitudes of native peoples—some friendly, others hostile, some inscrutably in-between—that he appears not to have taken the lack of welcome seriously. Perhaps he was feeling a bit indomitable. He had, after all, survived shipwreck, disease, starvation, thirst, and innumerable skirmishes and stand-offs, and had made one of the greatest odysseys in human history. He was no longer a wretched slave but a celebrated shaman and an imperial plenipotentiary. He refused to be refused by Hawikuh's leaders and insisted on approaching the city, but before he reached its walls, archers sallied forth and killed him and three hundred of his followers.

Fray Marcos reported that, when he heard the news of Estebanico's death, he hurried forward but stopped short of trying to enter Hawikuh. He was "satiated with fear" and did no more than glimpse the terraced stone city from across the plains. His impression was that it was "bigger than the city of Mexico." It wasn't. From a distance the seven cities of Cíbola might have looked like sprawling metropolises to a weary and traumatized friar, but they were only modest pueblos scattered along the Zuni River Basin in what is today western New Mexico.

Nevertheless, the tantalizing prospect of more rich kingdoms to investigate and conquer led to a massive reconnaissance that left from Compostela the next year, 1540, under the command of Francisco Vázquez de Coronado. Coronado was thirty years old, the beneficiary of a noble birth and an even nobler marriage to a woman whose father was said to be the illegitimate son of King Ferdinand. He was also the protégé of Viceroy Mendoza and had recently replaced Nuño de Guzmán as governor of Nueva Galicia. His *entrada* was a swarming mass of humans and livestock: thousands of cattle, sheep, and hogs to feed an expeditionary force made up of between three and four hundred Spanish soldiers, probably an equal number of slaves and servants, and an accompanying army of thousands of *indios amigos*, native allies from various Mexican tribes, armed with obsidian-edged swords and feather-work shields.

When Coronado reached Hawikuh, he ordered the *Requerimiento* read aloud to the Zuni-speaking warriors behind the city walls. The *Requerimiento* was a document created by pedantic legal minds back in Castile to provide a veneer of justification for the seizing of native lands and people. It offered a summary of the creation of the world, including the story of Adam and Eve, and told how God had bestowed ecclesiastical authority upon Saint Peter, and how Peter's successor as pontiff had granted the land upon which the Indians were living to Spain. "You can inspect the documents," the Zunis were told, "that recorded this grant." They were exhorted to "recognize the Church as owner and administrator of the entire world," and if they complied, they would receive various unspecified benefits.

However, if you do not do what I ask . . . I assure you that, with the help of God, I will attack you mightily . . . I will take your wives and children, and I will make them slaves . . . I declare that the deaths and injuries that occur as a result of this would be your fault and not His Majesty's, nor ours, nor that of these gentlemen who have come with me.

After the Zunis heard this incomprehensible pronouncement and "refused to have peace," Coronado and his Spanish men-at-arms and Indian allies attacked, overrunning and capturing the city. They eventually moved on to another complex of pueblos called Tiguex near modern-day Albuquerque and spent the winter fighting a brief, savage war with the Tiwa people who lived there. It was while he was in Tiguex that Coronado met the Turk, so named because his features reminded the Spaniards of their Old World Ottoman enemies. Nobody thought to record the Turk's real name, but he was the man who, thirteen years after the remnants of Narváez's expedition washed ashore on Galveston Island, was responsible for bringing Europeans back onto Texas soil.

The Turk was a member of an unknown tribe far to the east. He had been captured and enslaved at some point before Coronado's *entrada* by the people of Cicique, a populous pueblo eighty or ninety miles northeast of Tiguex, near present-day Santa Fe. What the Turk told the expeditionaries made them forget how lackluster the Seven Cities of Cibola had turned out to be. There was another place, he said, called Quivira, where there was a great river six miles across, with fish swimming in it that were the size of the Spaniards' horses, and where the rulers cruised along in ships with eagle figureheads fashioned out of gold and drifted to sleep beneath the forest canopy to the music of golden wind chimes. Coronado wasn't gullible, but he was intrigued enough to allow the Turk, when the spring came, to lead his expedition toward the hypnotic immensity of land that lay beyond the Pecos River.

This region was what would become known as the Texas Panhandle or, more lyrically, the Llano Estacado. Llano Estacado translates to "Staked Plains" or "Palisaded Plains." The term probably has to do with the stockade-like appearance of the eroded rock where the landscape east of Lubbock and Amarillo drops down suddenly from the table-land of the High Plains. A less likely explanation, but a more colorful and persistent one, refers to the wooden stakes that Coronado's men supposedly drove into the ground to create a trail they could follow across an utterly featureless grassland void. There is no mention of this particular breadcrumb trail in any of the expedition reports, but the vanguard of the army would sometimes leave piles of bones and cow dung to mark the way for those following behind.

———

The haunting monotony of the Llano made a deep impression. There were, Coronado wrote, "no more landmarks than as if we had been swallowed up in the sea . . . There was not a stone, nor a bit of rising ground, nor a tree, nor a shrub, nor anything to go by." One of the soldiers on the expedition, Pedro de Castañeda, was an especially close and curious observer of this unsettling environment and the effect it had on human perception.

The country is like a bowl, so that when a man sits down, the horizon surrounds him all around at the distance of a musket shot. There are no groves of trees except at the rivers, which flow at the bottom of some ravines where the trees grow so thick that they were not noticed until one was right on the edge of them. They are of dead earth.

But this seemingly blank world teemed with life, with vast prairie dog towns, and pale wraith-like wolves, and "foolish" rabbits that could not seem to evade the lances of the Spanish horsemen. Yet the strangest and most unforgettable creatures they encountered were the buffalo, the same shaggy "cows" that Cabeza de Vaca had seen years earlier when he was a traveling salesman on the coastal prairies. Now, amazed Spanish eyes saw them again. The animals traveled in herds so extensive that in weeks of travel the expedition never lost sight of them. "The country they traveled over," marveled Castañeda, "was so level and smooth that if one looked at them the sky could be seen between their legs, so that if some of them were at a distance they looked like smooth-trunked pines whose tops joined."

There were other humans on the plains as well, a nomadic tribe called the Querechos who hunted the bison and "lived like Arabs" in temporary encampments, teams of dogs hauling their goods and hide tents on travois from one place on the Llano to the next. The Querechos would become better known as a division of the Apaches, the Athapaskan-speaking people who for generations had been migrating southward on the Great Plains.

Along with the Comanches, they would evolve into iconic horseback warriors, but in 1541 the horses that accompanied the Coronado expedition were the first such animals they had ever seen.

The Querechos hunted buffalo for their own subsistence, but were also traders who were at that point making their presence felt in a thriving exchange network that linked the terraced pueblos of New Mexico with the woodland cultures of East Texas and beyond. Specifically, they were muscling in on the hide trade of another plains people, the Teyas, whom the Spaniards encountered when they entered the veinous network of canyon lands that occasionally provided a shock of scenery when glimpsed from the flat surface of the Llano. The Teyas warned Coronado that they knew all about Quivira, and that it was not an imposing city at all but a place of "straw and skins."

The Spaniards, their *indios amigos*, and the animals they herded along with them suffered constantly from thirst; there was no water on the Llano except for buffalo wallows and evaporating playa lakes that were sometimes covered with a thick rime of salt. A devastating hailstorm injured many of the expedition's horses, broke all the crockery, and left the camp in tatters. Nevertheless, Coronado was not going to go all that way without getting at least a glimpse of Quivira. He ordered the greater part of his army back to Tiguex and pressed ahead with thirty horsemen and a half-dozen foot soldiers, accompanied by Teyas guides and with the increasingly suspect Turk now under armed guard. It took them six weeks to reach their goal. The province of Quivira was as unimpressive as the Teyas had warned it would be, just a scattering of villages of grass houses out on the Kansas plains.

The Turk admitted, probably as he was being tortured, that he had misled the expedition on orders from the pueblo leaders back in Cicique, who wanted to see Coronado and his invaders as far away as possible, until they starved or died of thirst or became forever lost out on the inhospitable Llano. The Spaniards also suspected him of trying to stir up the people of Quivira into an attack. Coronado ordered that justice be administered, and left it to his *maestre de campo* to arrange the details. A soldier named Pérez crept up on the Turk from behind, slipped a cord over his neck, and strangled him by tightening the cord with a stick.

After that Coronado took his reconnaissance party back to Tiguex, where the rest of the army had withdrawn for the winter. There were plans to return to the plains in the spring, to keep pushing farther east despite the dispiriting results so far, but new crises intervened. A native insurrection in the south suddenly threatened the expedition's supply line to New Spain, and Coronado suffered a serious head trauma when the cinch strap of his saddle broke and sent him tumbling beneath the hooves of a comrade's galloping horse. After that, writes his biographer Herbert E. Bolton, "the real Coronado was no more." He was confused and cautious and his passion for exploration and conquest had dimmed. He recalled the predictions of a "scientific friend" of his back in Salamanca who said that he would one day become a powerful lord in distant

———

lands, but that he would suffer a fall from which he would never recover. "This expectation of death," Castañeda writes, "made him desire to return and die where he had a wife and children."

Coronado lived for twelve more years after returning to Mexico as the leader of a failed and expensive expedition, one that for all its far-ranging investigations into Texas had found very little in terms of real material wealth. He was beset in his last years by charges of bribery and corruption and was forced to step down as the governor of Nueva Galicia. The year before he died, he became a target of reformers whose consciences were inflamed by the atrocities committed by the rulers of New Spain. He was tried—but acquitted—on various counts of cruelty and abuse to the inhabitants of Tierra Nueva, including burning thirty people at the stake during the Tiguex War, setting dogs on others, and murdering the Turk.

✝

AS CORONADO, IN HIS CONCUSSED and fatalistic state, was leading his men back to Mexico in 1542, another Spanish expedition was in the process of unraveling a thousand miles to the east. Hernando de Soto, an adventurer who had made his enormous fortune and reputation in the conquest of the Incas, and who had been awarded the imperial contract to explore and conquer—where Narváez had failed—the vast territory from Florida to Pánuco, was dying in a brush house in the Indian kingdom of Guachoya somewhere in southeastern Arkansas. Guachoya was one of many native principalities that de Soto had attacked, courted, or intimidated in his grueling three-year reconnaissance of the southeast quadrant of North America. He had fought many battles as he and his six hundred men marched from one Indian capital to the next, searching for the new Tenochtitlán that was

———

certain to lie just beyond the next river. They had deployed their horses to powerful strategic effect, running down and lancing the Indian warriors who opposed them. They had routinely taken chieftains hostage, enslaved their subjects, cut off the hands and noses of Indians they suspected of duplicity. Others they had burned alive or fed to their voracious war dogs.

They had wandered from Florida swamps to Appalachian forests, through a country vastly different and far more populated than the treeless emptiness Coronado had encountered on the South Plains of Texas. Instead of pueblos and nomadic camps, there were consolidated metropolitan districts ruled over by powerful chieftains, some of them female, and cities and ceremonial centers dominated by temple mounds and guarded by palisade walls.

But there was no gold, only endless rumors of it, enticing the Spaniards ever deeper into the heart of the continent. They had done little to make themselves welcome, and after three years of constant warfare and hardship, almost half of them were dead, and most of their horses too. De Soto's own journey came to an end on the western side of the Mississippi. He "sank into a deep despondency" when he realized the extent of the impassable terrain that separated him from the Gulf Coast, where he had hoped to build ships to sail the survivors of his expedition to Mexico or Cuba. His health collapsed along with his spirits. As he lay dying of fever on his pallet, he committed his soul to God and appointed Luis de Moscoso to succeed him. Moscoso was thirty-seven. He had fought alongside de Soto in Peru and had served as his chief subordinate during the embattled and disastrous trek through La Florida.

Among Moscoso's first decisions as the new governor of this decidedly unconquered region was to exhume his predecessor's body almost as soon as it was buried. He needed to keep de Soto's death a secret from the people of Guachoya, with whom the Spaniards had only a tremulous alliance. In the will that de Soto had made in Havana before his fleet sailed, he had stipulated that his body be buried in his homeland of Extremadura, in a chapel built especially to receive it, whose walls would bear his family's coat of arms and whose altar would be decorated with the cross of the order of the Knights of Santiago. But in the end he was interred in a tomb of moving water. His remains were wrapped in a shawl, weighted with sand, and deposited into the Mississippi.

Moscoso's worn-out and disillusioned men were ready to go home, and so was he. "The Governor," one chronicler of the expedition recalled, "longed to be again where he could get his full measure of sleep." From the Mississippi the remains of the *entrada* headed west, believing they would find their way to Mexico and Spanish civilization. The way forward led them across the Red River and into the rolling grasslands and woodlands of East Texas, the land of the Caddos. Like many of the other Indians de Soto and his men had encountered, the Caddos were a settled agricultural people with a complex political system of towns and villages confederated into chiefdoms. They built temple mounds, lived in tall conical houses amid extensive cornfields, and worshipped a deity they called "Leader Up Above." The Caddos had heard all about the depredations of the foreign intruders coming from the east and rose up against them, but Moscoso and his men continued to fight their way forward, winning pitched battles, burning down villages, and seizing Indians to serve as guides and hostages. They reached a river named the Daycao—which could have been the Trinity, or the Navasota, or possibly the Brazos—before realizing they had to turn back. Winter was coming, the country was growing more rugged and inhospitable, and the hope of finding a Spanish outpost in this direction was proving to be a dream.

So Moscoso ordered a retreat all the way to the Mississippi. The Spaniards backtracked through lands they had already despoiled, facing ambushes from the same people they had already fought, who were enraged by their reappearance. Four hundred miles upriver from the Gulf of Mexico, they spent the winter of 1542–1543 doing the same thing that Narváez had done fourteen years earlier: building boats. Salvation lay seaward, down the Mississippi, around the westward curve of the gulf to the same Spanish outpost of Pánuco. The Spaniards built seven flat-bottomed, barge-like vessels that they spent seventeen days rowing down the river. They covered the sides of the boats with thick fiber mats for protection against enemy arrows, and towed lashed-together dugout canoes in which their few remaining horses teetered.

Moscoso and his men were attacked along the way by fleets of Indian canoes, leading to pitched naval battles in the middle of the Mississippi and to harrying attacks that continued almost all the way to the mouth of the river. They headed toward the open sea at first, but they were short on water and the boats were leaky, so they sailed inland and hugged the coast, rowing hard against contrary winds that threatened on some days to drive them back out to sea, on others to send them crashing onto the shore.

After a ten-day voyage westward from the mouth of the Mississippi, the Spaniards were introduced to the abundant discomforts of the Texas coast. One night they were blown toward shore, dragging their improvised anchors, along a desolate stretch of exposed beach. They were probably not far from where the remnants of Narváez's expedition had washed ashore, maybe even on the same island of Malhado. They had the advantage of not making landfall on a fierce winter day as Cabeza de Vaca had, but the summer wind, howling in from the south, was such a threat that half of the men had to jump into the shallow water and point the bows of the boats into the gale to keep them from being swamped. They did that all night long, and in the morning, when the wind finally died down, there was such a dense congregation of mosquitoes that they covered the white sails of the boats and turned them black. The men were so tormented by mosquito bites, one of them later wrote, "they could but laugh."

But this otherwise inhospitable coast had at

———

least one welcome feature. There was a dark viscous "scum" seeping up from the sea floor that the voyagers employed to seal the leaky gaps in the planking of their boats. It was the same substance that coastal Indians painted onto their pots for decorative effect. It would be another few centuries before a more crucial purpose would be found for Texas oil.

Their boats patched, their water casks filled, Moscoso and his men embarked in a cloud of mosquitoes and sailed south along the Texas coast in high summer. They stayed generally seaward of the barrier islands and their treacherous rows of offshore sandbars, though they cautiously entered the bays and lagoons to set nets for fish and to dig in the sand for more fresh water. Fifty-two days after embarking from the mouth of the Mississippi, they finally made it to Pánuco, the Spanish settlement that the doomed Narváez expedition was never destined to reach.

The surviving half of the de Soto expedition had managed to escape Texas without running aground or starving to death or being killed by its aggrieved inhabitants. But for many years to come the low-lying coast, assaulted by storms in summer and winter, with no landmarks except shifting dune fields, remained a lethal barrier to any secure European foothold in Texas.

✚

W OE TO US WHO ARE GOING TO Spain," a priest named Juan Ferrer supposedly prophesied before embarking from the Mexican port of Veracruz a decade after Moscoso's homemade ships came limping back to Spanish territory, "because neither we nor the fleet will arrive there. Most of us will perish, and those who are left will experience great torment, though all will die in the end except a very few."

Fray Ferrer and four other Dominican clerics were among the four hundred passengers who left

―――

the shores of Mexico for Spain in April of 1554. They traveled in a fleet of four ships, bearing the wealth of New Spain back to its mother country and into the imperial treasury of Charles V. Most of this wealth was in the form of gold and silver from the mines of northern Mexico, the Crown's share stored in dozens of custom-designed trunks. There was a great deal of coinage as well, minted in Mexico City, that represented the private fortunes of merchants and individual passengers headed home to Spain, or the legacies and bequests of men who had died in the conquest. Included in the cargo were other New World products such as cowhides, resin, cochineal, silk thread, and sugar.

The ships were to stop in Havana before crossing the Atlantic, but they were still far from Cuba when a powerful spring storm erupted in the gulf. One of the ships managed to escape, but the other three were driven westward and broke apart on the shores of what is now called Padre Island. Padre is the longest of the barrier islands that shadow the Texas coast and an even worse place to be shipwrecked

than the Narváez expedition's fatal island of Malhado, which is farther north and east. Padre is a
113-mile-long stretch of tidal flats and wind-scoured
dunes, separated from the mainland along its whole
length by a forbidding saltwater lagoon.

The details of what exactly happened to the
three hundred or so survivors of the shipwreck
are hazy, but there is no doubt that the apocalyptic
predictions of Fray Ferrer were largely borne out.
Although it appears that several dozen castaways
managed to salvage one of the ships' boats and sail
it back to Veracruz with news of the disaster, the
rest of the men, women, and children stranded on
the forsaken beach decided that their best hope
for survival was to walk south along the coast.
Like the unfortunate members of the Narváez and
de Soto expeditions before them, they would try
to reach Pánuco. But after twenty days at sea in
hostile weather, driven all over the western gulf by
uncertain winds, they were severely disoriented.
They thought they were much farther south than
they really were, and that a march of two or three

days would deliver them from the wilderness, but in fact they were over three hundred miles from Pánuco: three hundred miles of barren sand, boggy marshlands, tangled mangrove swamps, and broad rivers they had no means to cross.

They had been walking for a week when they encountered Indians. These people may have been a division of the Karankawas, or perhaps one of the other tribes Cabeza de Vaca had encountered on his own march south from Malhado. According to an account set down forty years later by a priest who claimed to have interviewed one of the party's two survivors, the Indians brought food and made signs of peace. Something in their demeanor, though, must have made the Spaniards nervous. As they sat down to eat their first meal in a week, they gripped their sabers and readied the two crossbows they had managed to salvage from the wrecks. While they were eating, their hosts attacked. The castaways managed to drive them away without suffering any immediate casualties, but the skirmish was only a prelude to a hellish retreat.

———

The survivors of the shipwrecks continued marching down the coast as the Indians followed, killing stragglers with arrows while the main party stumbled blindly south. Harassed every step of the way, with nothing to eat and nothing to drink except the dew they were able to lick from the dune grasses, they managed to make it fifty miles to the southern tip of Padre Island, where their way was barred by the mouth of the Rio Grande emptying into the sea. They lashed driftwood rafts together with cord they had carried from the wrecks and crossed precariously to the other side. They lost their two crossbows in the middle of the river and came to shore again virtually defenseless and still at the mercy of their pursuers, possibly the same Indians that had followed them along the length of Padre Island but more likely another tribe that had taken up the relay mission of annihilating the intruders.

Because the Indians soon stripped the clothes off two of the Spaniards without killing them, the castaways allowed themselves to hope that if they threw off their own ragged garments, they would be left alone. Under the crushing burden of sixteenth-century Catholic shame, they made their way forward naked. The lone (and at least somewhat dubious) chronicler of the disaster wrote that several of the women died of embarrassment, "helpless to protect the decency that normally would be bought at the cost of one's life."

In order to preserve some scrap of modesty, the priests sent the women and children ahead in a kind of vanguard, where they could remain out of sight. But by the time the men caught up with them on the banks of Mexico's Rio de las Palmas, they were all dead, killed by native arrows. By this point there were something like two hundred survivors of the shipwreck left, all of them men, five of them priests. Fifty were killed after they crossed the river, the rest one by one or in small groups as they staggered onward toward Pánuco. One of the two ultimate survivors was Francisco Vázquez, who somehow backtracked alone all the way to the shipwreck site, where he was rescued by a ship that had been sent to search for the lost fleet. The other was one of the priests, Fray Marcos de Mena, who, despite suffering from seven maggot-infested arrow wounds, managed to make his way at last to Pánuco and astound the residents of a Spanish house when he knocked on their front door.

By that point, or shortly after, a salvage fleet was already on the way from Veracruz to recover the boxes of bullion and coinage that had been lost when the ships broke apart and sank in the Texas surf, money that the aging Charles V acutely needed to fight the latest of his chronic wars with France. Much of the treasure—perhaps half of it— was brought up by divers, but the rest was buried and scattered by months, and then years, and then centuries of ceaseless wind and waves. The silver *reales*—covered with tar, worn thin as communion wafers—still wash up on the Padre Island beach.

The Spanish presence in Texas had by now run aground as surely as had its treasure fleet. The Narváez expedition was a gruesome failure that gave rise to chimerical stories of golden cities, luring Coronado out onto the empty buffalo plains

---

and sending him home a ruined man. Moscoso, in his sally into Texas after de Soto's death, found nothing to conquer but much to destroy. With the loss of the treasure fleet added to this list of disasters, it was no accident that Texas found its way to the bottom of New Spain's priority list of territorial ambition. The wave of conquest lapped briefly over the Rio Grande, then receded for decades. The urgency to explore a region that seemed to offer very little was gone, especially after silver was discovered in Zacatecas in 1546, sparking a mining boom and a fierce decades-long war with the Chichimeca peoples of northern Mexico. But the vast Texas unknown was still there, and the European hunger for its domination had not gone away.

✝

S OR MARÍA DE JESÚS DE ÁGREDA, THE abbess of the Convent of the Immaculate Conception, was forty-eight years old in the winter of 1650. She had lived her whole life in Ágreda, a village in northeastern Spain at the base of the Iberian Cordillera. It had been a life of spiritual wonder and turmoil, marked by ecstatic visions but also by horrible doubts and temptations. As a child she had watched her mother meditate on mortality in front of a human skull. She had woken at three in the morning to the sound of her devout father shuffling along the floor under the weight of a hundred-pound iron cross. Suffering and mortification, she understood, were what led a soul into the presence of God. When she entered the convent at eighteen, she slept two hours a day on the hardest surface she could find, grudgingly ate a few vegetables for the sake of staying alive, and petitioned her superior for a habit made of coarser cloth.

———

But there were lingering concerns about Sor María, concerns that the Holy Office of the Inquisition felt the need to investigate. They wanted to know more about her mystical revelations, the claims that she levitated during prayer, and above all her mysterious *exterioridades* in which she was said to exist in two places at the same time.

It was a January day. Sor María was so weak with fever she could not walk, and had to be carried down from the infirmary to the library where the interrogation was to take place. No allowances were made for her illness. To protect their isolation, the cloistered nuns at the convent usually spoke with visitors through a grillwork covered with projecting spikes. But Sor María was instructed to kneel at a communion rail and answer her examiner, a priest named Antonio Gonzalo del Moral, face to face.

In the presence of a notary, Moral began assaulting the abbess with questions as she struggled to remain conscious and upright on the communion rail. Most of the questions had to do with something that began happening three decades earlier, when the young Sor María claimed that—while her body remained in the convent in Ágreda—she crossed the Atlantic and appeared "in the kingdoms of Quivira and the Jumanas," preaching the Gospel to the pagan inhabitants of New Spain.

It was Moral's objective to determine if these "bilocations" were real, and if so, whether they were holy miracles or some sort of mischief stirred up by the Devil. Sor María's spirit journeys could not be dismissed out of hand. There was evidence that something of the sort had taken place.

By the first third of the 1600s, Texas was still little more than an enticing blank when it came to serious Spanish initiatives. But two expeditions had ventured north along the Rio Grande, into the Pueblo country of New Mexico, and helped to reignite the old dreams of golden or silver cities somewhere just over the horizon. In 1595, Juan de Oñate, married to a woman of noble Castilian and Aztec blood—a descendent of both Cortés and Moctezuma—followed up those scouting *entradas* with a much grander colonizing expedition, creating a line

———

73

of Spanish settlement along the upper Rio Grande. Here, beyond the western margins of Texas, among the Pueblo peoples whose existence had already been destabilized by Coronado, Franciscan friars with a fervent determination to Christianize the Indians had created a hardscrabble cluster of missions.

In 1629, a delegation of Jumano Indians appeared at one of these missions. They came from the east, from the Texas plains. The Jumanos were mostly a farming people, living in extensive villages of flat-roofed houses along the Rio Grande and in the fertile river juncture where the Rio Grande met the Conchos, known to the Spanish as La Junta de los Ríos. But this band lived much farther north. They hunted buffalo on the vast grasslands, and played a vibrant role in the trading economy that had developed among the Spanish newcomers and the multitudes of indigenous tribes that lived far to the east of the mission outposts in New Mexico.

The Jumano delegation told the friars that they wanted missionaries to come with them to their home territory, to live with them and establish missions and baptize them as Christians. They said that for a number of years they had been receiving mysterious visitations from a woman who was young and beautiful and spoke their language. She was barefoot and wore a gray sackcloth habit and a heavy blue cloak. This "Lady in Blue," they said, visited the Indians hundreds of times, preaching to them about Christ and the Trinity, imploring them to seek out the friars who could bring them into the light of salvation.

The Franciscans were excited by the spectacle of these tattooed visitors appearing from the wilderness, after apparently having experienced a spontaneous conversion by what could only have been a blessed apparition. Two friars were assigned to accompany the Jumanos back to the buffalo plains, to assess the feasibility of building a mission in the heart of the little-known country that lay north and east of the line of Spanish settlement.

The tough priests who trekked three hundred miles through the summer heat to visit the

Jumanos in their homeland were greeted with jubilation, though the mission they hoped to build never got further than the planning stages. The Indians may indeed have had a cultural epiphany prompted by the appearance of a bilocating Spanish nun, but that didn't rule out a more pragmatic strategy. The Jumanos of the plains were in trouble. The Apaches, rising in power, were raiding down from the north and threatening the Jumanos' control of the buffalo grounds and lucrative trading routes. A Spanish mission would have meant not just priests but soldiers, the beginning of an alliance against a powerful enemy. But the Jumanos lived far away from the Spanish outposts, and the country between was so vast and inhospitable that the alliance never happened.

It was twenty years later that Father Moral began to question María de Ágreda, and by then the Jumanos had surrendered the plains to the Apaches. They had retreated to the farming pueblos along the rivers and had begun to melt into history. But the question of whether a Lady in Blue had actually appeared to them was still of acute interest to the Inquisition.

Moral questioned the abbess unrelentingly, three hours a day for eleven days as she kneeled at the communion rail. When she returned from her first miraculous journey to the New World, had she told her confessor what had happened? Had she indeed flown to that region on the wings of St. Michael the Archangel? What places did she see as she was being transported across the world? When it rained in the kingdoms she visited, were her clothes wet when she returned? How did she carry physical objects like rosaries to the Indians? What was their language like? What sort of weapons did they have? What happened to her body in the convent while she was preaching to the Indians on the other side of the ocean? Did an angel inhabit it so that she could continue performing her duties as abbess?

Sor María never objected to any of these questions nor tried to evade them. Ill and uncomfortable as she was, she answered everything with striking patience and candor. She was much older than she had been when her mysterious travels began, and she testified honestly that she did not know exactly what had happened, whether she had actually been carried by angels to rescue the souls of people in faraway lands or, in her zeal and youthful confusion, only thought that she had. All she knew for certain was that her *exterioridades* were not the work of the Devil.

Moral agreed. He was moved by her obvious devotion, her "sublime holiness." "I say that she is a catholic and faithful Christian," he concluded in his report to the inquisitor-general, "well-founded in our holy faith. She embroidered no fiction into her accounts, nor was she deluded by the devil."

The abbess was judged to be authentic, but the land she claimed to have visited might still have seemed to her inquisitors as the projection of a mind inflamed. She had mentioned numerous Indian nations besides the Jumanos to whom she had appeared, though she couldn't vouch for having their names right. Among these people were the Cambujos, the Chillescas, and the Titlas, who lived in the forested realms of the east. In Sor María's telling, they were reminiscent of the fantastical sophisticated Indian kingdoms like Quivira that had once lured Coronado, places of wealth and glorious indolence longing to be shown the path to God.

Texas at this time was hardly a void. It was peopled in its north and west by a swirling complex of nomadic buffalo-hunting tribes like the Teyas and Apaches and plains Jumanos; by the settled agricultural branches of the Jumanos at the Junta de los Ríos where the Rio Grande met the Conchos; by the Coahulitecans of the southern prairies and the Karankawas along the Gulf Coast; and by the various extensive Caddo tribes in the eastern forests gathered into the Hasinai Confederacy. But the strangers who had come from across the sea to the New World over a hundred years before still knew very little about it. From a European perspective it remained largely unseen and unsettled, a speculatively rendered immensity on a series of inaccurate maps. To the mind of a brilliant and confused young nun who had never left her village in Spain, it was more than that—it was a shining emptiness that had the power to lure her away and liberate her from her cloistered body.

At the time Sor María was being questioned by the Inquisition, Spain had been hovering at the edges of this Texas mirage for a hundred years, with no mercenary reason or national rivalry strong enough to warrant any serious further explorations beyond the Rio Grande. Coronado had proved only that the golden cities did not exist, and Moscoso had triggered unrelenting hostility but found nothing worth fighting for. For the castaways of the Spanish treasure fleet of 1554, Texas was almost literally a hell. But it was also a place from which the Spanish mind could not release its material dreams, its mystical claims. No matter how blank Texas was, no matter how bleak, Spain was not going to give it away without a fight.

———

SOME SUGGESTIONS
FOR FURTHER READING

Barr, Juliana. *Peace Came in the Form of a Woman: Indians and Spaniards in the Texas Borderlands.* Chapel Hill: University of North Carolina Press, 2007.

Bolton, Herbert E. *Coronado: Knight of Pueblos and Plains.* Reprint. Albuquerque: University of New Mexico Press, 1990.

———. *Spanish Exploration in the Southwest: 1542–1706.* New York: Charles Scribner's Sons, 1916.

Cabeza de Vaca, Álvar Núñez. *The Narrative of Cabeza de Vaca.* Edited, translated, and with an introduction by Rolena Adorno and Patrick Charles Pautz. Lincoln: University of Nebraska Press, 2003.

———

Chipman, Donald E., and Harriett Denis Joseph. *Spanish Texas, 1519–1821: Revised Edition*. Austin: University of Texas Press, 2010.

Fedewa, Marilyn H. *María of Ágreda: Mystical Lady in Blue*. Albuquerque: University of New Mexico Press, 2010.

Flint, Richard. *No Settlement, No Conquest: A History of the Coronado Entrada*. Albuquerque: University of New Mexico Press, 2008.

Goodwin, Robert. *Crossing the Continent, 1527–1540: The Story of the First African-American Explorer of the American South*. New York: Harper Collins, 2008.

Hanke, Lewis. *All Mankind Is One: A Study of the Disputation between Bartolomé de Las Casas and Juan Ginés de Sepúlveda in 1550 on the Religious and Intellectual Capacity of the American Indians*. DeKalb: Northern Illinois University Press, 1974.

Hickerson, Nancy Parrott. *The Jumanos: Hunters and Traders of the South Plains*. Austin: University of Texas Press, 1994.

Hodge, Frederick W., and Theodore H. Lewis, eds. *Spanish Explorers in the Southern United States, 1528–1543*. Austin: Texas State Historical Association, 1984.

Hudson, Charles. *Knights of Spain, Warriors of the Sun: Hernando de Soto and the South's Ancient Chiefdoms*. Athens: University of Georgia Press, 1997.

La Vere, David. *The Texas Indians*. College Station: Texas A&M University Press, 2003.

———

Newcomb, W. W., Jr. *The Indians of Texas: From Prehistoric to Modern Times*. Austin: University of Texas Press, 1972.

Reséndez, Andrés. *A Land So Strange*. New York: Basic Books, 2007.

Ricklis, Robert A. *The Karankawa Indians of Texas: An Ecological Study of Cultural Tradition and Change*. Austin: University of Texas Press, 1996.

Schneider, Paul. *Brutal Journey: Cabeza de Vaca and the Epic First Crossing of North America*. New York: Henry Holt, 2006.

Turner, Ellen Sue, and Thomas R. Hester. *Stone Artifacts of Texas Indians*. 3rd ed. Dallas: Taylor Trade Publishing, 2011.

Shafer, Harry J. *Painters in Prehistory: Archeology and Art of the Lower Pecos Canyonlands*. San Antonio: Trinity University Press, 2013.

Weber, David. *The Spanish Frontier in North America*. New Haven: Yale University Press, 1992.

Weddle, Robert S. *Spanish Sea*. College Station: Texas A&M University Press, 1985.